To Matthew, Molly, Calvin, and Rowen
There will always be someone that loves you,
no matter how bad your day is.

LCCN: 2014910905   Copyright ©2014 by Debbie Reece

ISBN 978-0-692-23084-8

The Worst Day Ever!

By Debbie Reece
Illustrated by Ron Head

Thank you Mom, Dad, and Eddy,
for patience and love.
Thank you Ron, for bringing this
story to life through
your illustrations.

James loves going to school. He has two best friends, Molly and Will. They are in the same class, share the same lunchtime, and play together at recess. School is fun for James until one day when everything seems to go wrong. Could this be the worst day ever?

It was a fresh spring morning. The sun was shining and James was eager to get to school. He gave his mother a hug, found his friends, Molly and Will, and hopped on the colored tiles down the hall to the classroom.

"I hope we play tag in gym today," Will whispered to James while the teacher placed the chairs in a semi-circle. Instead, it was music in the classroom. During the lesson, they decided to pretend-wrestle in their chairs. Suddenly, James toppled onto the floor! "James," his teacher scolded, "this is not gym class.

Did you leave your good behavior at home today?" He tried to explain, but it was too late. She was already writing his name on the board in front of the classroom for everyone to see.

After a morning of music and reading, his teacher gave the class some free time.

They were playing tic-tac-toe when Michael teased, "Nine, ten, say it again! James has a big, fat head!" James felt a little confused and hurt. Michael had never been mean like that before.

During the morning restroom break, James looked in the mirror. He was sure he had his good behavior with him. He didn't notice the tiny, gray cloud above his head.

The scent of tater tots led the class,
single file, down the hall to lunch. Except
for James, he liked to zigzag hop on the
colored tiles.

After two warnings, the teacher put a mark next to his name for
poor hallway behavior. He tried to explain, but it was too late.
She had already made the mark on her clipboard.

While James and his friends were eating lunch, they started acting silly. He was bopping them on the nose with his milk carton when they noticed the lunch-lady standing next to their table.

Her apron said "HELPER" but they had a funny feeling she was not going to be very helpful. "James," she scolded, "you are acting too silly."

She pulled a card from her apron and instructed, "Give this to your teacher." He tried to explain, but it was too late. She had already given him the dreaded black lunch card.

On the way back to class, James went to the restroom and looked in the mirror. This time he saw a small, gloomy cloud over his head. It matched the way he was feeling.

He walked down the hall silent and single file. He handed the black lunch card to his teacher and watched as she put a second mark next to his name on the board in front of the classroom for everyone to see. He sighed, "Maybe recess will make this a better day."

"RECESS!" The class roared. They burst through the doors to the playground. James ran to play with Molly and Will. "James," the teacher reminded him, "I am sorry, but you must wait five minutes because your name and two marks are on the board."

After five long minutes, he raced over to play with Will. Molly saw him and teased, "James! I'm going to tell the teacher you hit me!" He felt a little confused and hurt. He had not hit her AND he was afraid his teacher would put another mark next to his name on the board in front of the classroom for everyone to see.

That afternoon, James went back to the restroom and looked in the mirror. This time he saw a large, dark storm cloud over his head. It matched the way he felt.

For the rest of the day, he tried to do his work. All he could think about was his name on the board, with two marks next to it.

The dismissal bell finally rang. The students rushed to the door through a maze of tables and chairs. When the teacher asked the class to line up, Max made a sneaky face and jumped right in front of James.

James marched outside to find his mother.

"Why do you look so mad?" she asked. "Max jumped in front of me in line," he growled. Kneeling down, she gave him a hug and looked in his folder.

She saw the notes from his teacher and whispered, "Looks like you had a bad day." It was all he could do to get into the car before the storm cloud over his head burst.

On the way home, he told his mother about his day.

He explained that it was Will's idea to play and he got in trouble.

He said they were all being silly at lunch and he got a black lunch card.

She tried to explain that it was not fair to blame others, but he was not listening.

He told her Michael teased him in the classroom...

...and Molly picked on him at recess.

"This was the worst day EVER!" he shouted and flopped back in his seat like a worn rag doll.

In the rear view mirror, she could see his face in his hands as he whimpered, "And I just know...sniffle... that when we get home.... sniffle...you won't even want to hug me."

"It sounds like you had a pretty bad day. Why don't you meet me at our favorite chair?" his mother softly said.

He crawled into her lap. She gave him a warm hug. She spoke with a soothing voice, "I will always love you and hug you, no matter how bad your day is. That's what mothers do." James smiled and whispered, "I love you mom." She whispered, "I love you too."

He relaxed, wrapped in his mother's hug, for a long time.

That evening, during dinner, James told his father about his day.
They talked about the school rules and ways to make better choices.

When his mother tucked him into bed she said, "Maybe Michael was having a bad day and someone gave him a hug too."

That night James dreamed about playing with his friends.

A few weeks later James and his friends were eating lunch, and acting silly, when they noticed the lunch-lady standing next to their table, again. This time she handed the dreaded black lunch card to Molly.

Her eyes welled up with tears. She had never been in trouble at school. James leaned over, put his arm around her and whispered...

"It's okay, I know there is someone at home that will always love you and hug you, no matter how bad your day is."

How does a hug feel to you?

Use this page to describe how a hug feels to you. Share it with us on Facebook at BeeBopBooks and at www.beebopbooks.com. You can send it to us and we will display it on our website. Share your story today.

Mail it to:
BeeBop Books
PO Box 1424
Howe, TX 75459